Design Explorations
for the CREATIVE QUILTER

EASY-TO-FOLLOW LESSONS FOR DYNAMIC ART QUILTS

KATIE PASQUINI MASOPUST

Text and artwork copyright © 2008 by Katie Pasquini Masopust

Artwork copyright © 2008 by C&T Publishing, Inc.

Publisher: Amy Marson

Creative Director: Gailen Runge

Acquisitions Editor: Jan Grigsby

Editor: Lynn Koolish

Technical Editors: Sandy Peterson and Carolyn Aune

Copyeditor/Proofreader: Randalyn Perkins, Wordfirm Inc.

Cover Designer: Kristen Yenche

Design Director: Christina D. Jarumay

Book Designer: Kristy K. Zacharias

Page Layout Artist: AK Design

Production Coordinators: Matt Allen and Kirstie L. Pettersen

Illustrators: Richard Sheppard and Chris Pasquini

Photography by Luke Mulks and Diane Pedersen of C&T Publishing unless otherwise noted

Published by C&T Publishing, Inc., P.O. Box 1456, Lafayette, CA 94549

Library of Congress Cataloging-in-Publication Data

Pasquini Masopust, Katie.

Design explorations for the creative quilter : easy-to-follow lessons for dynamic art quilts / Katie Pasquini Masopust.

p. cm.

Includes index.

Summary: "Bring out your inner artist—explore 10 approaches to designing art quilts. Techniques work for everyone, beginner or advanced."—Provided by publisher.

ISBN 978-1-57120-455-4 (paper trade : alk. paper)

1. Quilting. 2. Art quilts--Design. I. Title.

TT835.P35193 2008

746.46'041--dc22

2008014577

Printed in China

10 9 8 7 6 5 4 3 2 1

Dedication

To my husband, who is the heart of my world.

Acknowledgments

SPECIAL THANKS TO THOSE CLOSE TO ME WHO HELPED CREATE THIS BOOK:

Brad—my computer technician

Natalia—my double solitaire buddy when I need to take a break

Randalyn—for using her own cropping tools to find the heart of my words

Chris—for his wonderful drawings

Cindy—for keeping me organized

I'd also like to thank my many students who helped me sort things out and who contributed the wonderful artwork produced as a result of their explorations.

CONTENTS

preface

I HAVE been making quilts for 30 years! I started by following traditional quilt patterns. My first quilt was a wedding present for my sister, Terry, with her new initial embroidered in the center block. Half-square triangles surrounded the center block, creating border after border until the quilt was bed size. The fabrics were scraps from the dresses our mother had sewn for us. The quilting should really be called basting, but I got better with practice. I was thrilled with every step in the process. I made several more traditional quilts, and then opened a quilt shop, which I ran for almost 5 years. I taught quilting classes and made my quilts.

In 1978, I attended a quilting conference and heard Michael James speak about his original art quilts. The lightbulb went on for me. I was inspired and began designing my own quilts. I had been a painter before I became a quilter, so I relied on my art knowledge to create these new quilts. My first art quilts were called mandalas. They were designed like kaleidoscopic images, with wedge shapes radiating out from the center. I enjoyed making mandalas for four years. I then began to play with three-dimensional designs that I remembered from a mechanical drawing class I had taken in high school, creating very dimensional, structural quilts. After exploring those for five years, I moved on to isometric perspective designs. These quilts are like baby-block patterns gone wild. What fun! I worked with the isometric grids for five years, and then we moved to New Mexico. My quilt designs began reflecting the landscapes around me. I drew from photographs. I fractured the surface to allow for value and color changes and to give the designs structure. That led me to adding watercolors and transparencies to my designs. In 2002, I started working with abstract designs, the subject of this book.

Terry and Jim Robertson's wedding quilt

This is the first quilt I made. I used a rainbow color scheme with a framed composition. The embroidered center R is surrounded by half-square triangles made from scraps of fabrics from the dresses my mother had made for Terry and me.

Redwood Forest by Katie Pasquini Masopust, 70" × 70", 2004

This ghost-layer and color-wash quilt uses colors from nature featuring the complementary colors of red and green in a vertical composition. A transparent forest floats in and out of the dominant trees. From The Hendricks Collection.